MONSTERS

ZOMBIES

By Cynthia Jenson-Elliott

KIDHAVEN PRESS

An imprint of Thomson Gale, a part of The Thomson Corporation

THOMSON

GALE

Detroit • New York • San Francisco • San Diego • New Haven, Conn.
Waterville, Maine • London • Munich

© 2007 Thomson Gale, a part of The Thomson Corporation.

Thomson and Star Logo are trademarks and Gale and KidHaven Press are registered trademarks used herein under license.

For more information, contact
KidHaven Press
27500 Drake Rd.
Farmington Hills, MI 48331-3535
Or you can visit our Internet site at http://www.gale.com

Every effort has been made to trace the owners of copyrighted material.

PICTURE CREDITS: Cover photo: Peter Iovino/Warner Bros./The Kobal Collection; Tony Arruza/CORBIS, 20; © Mihai Barbu/Reuters/CORBIS, 36; Thony Belizaire/AFP/Getty Images, 9; David M. Benett/Getty Images Entertainment/Getty Images, 39; Columbia Pictures/Photofest, 40; © Michael Gibson/Universal Pictures/ZUMA/CORBIS, 5, 6–7, 25; © Roger Hutchings/Alamy, 17, 21; © Images & Stories/Alamy, 12; Peter Iovino/Warner Bros./The Kobal Collection, 26; © Kelly-Mooney Photography/CORBIS, 14; Photos.com, 29 (top right, top left, lower left); Pictorial Parade/Hulton Archive/Getty Images, 35; Michael Rougier/Time & Life Pictures/Getty Images, 33; Dominic Rouse/The Image Bank/Getty Images, 16; © Les Stone/Sygma/CORBIS, 10–11; © Hans Strand/CORBIS, 30; Juan Carlos Ulate/Reuters/Landov, 18; United Film/The Kobal Collection, 24; Warner Bros./Photofest, 37; © Ken Wilson; Papilio/CORBIS, 29 (middle right)

LIBRARY OF CONGRESS CATALOGING-IN-PUBLICATION DATA

Jenson-Elliott, Cynthia
  Zombies / by Cynthia Jenson-Elliott.
    p. cm. — (Monsters)
  Includes bibliographical references and index.
  Contents: The living dead—Zombie tales—Zombies explained—Zombie fun.
  ISBN 0-7377-3557-0 (hard cover : alk. paper) 1. Zombies—Juvenile literature.
I. Title. II. Monsters (KidHaven Press)
  GR581.J46 2006
  398'.45—dc22
                                                              2006007123

Printed in the United States

CONTENTS

CHAPTER 1

THE LIVING DEAD

Zombies are dead people who have been brought back to life. They have been called many names—the living dead, the walking dead, and even the undead. Zombies are a lot like living people. They walk around, do work, wear clothes, and even, in some stories, eat and sleep. But in most stories and movies about them, zombies look more dead than alive—like people who have been rotting in a grave for a long time.

Zombies have skin that is very pale, the greenish gray color of moldy cheese. Their clothes are often torn. They look and smell like raw meat that has been left out for too long. They may have

4

The zombie character's skin is a sickening, greenish hue in this scene from Land of the Dead.

worms and maggots crawling out of open wounds in their flesh. Some zombies have body parts missing—eyes hanging out of their sockets, or arms chopped off at the elbow.

Zombies are not bothered by their wounds, however. That is because they do not feel any pain. Zombies do not feel anything at all, in fact. So, no matter how badly they are hurt, they just keep going, shuffling slowly along with staring eyes.

Their strange, blank faces and slow movements make zombies easy to recognize. Harold Courlander, a **folklorist** who studied in Haiti, the Caribbean nation where most zombie stories

In the movie Dawn of the Dead, *a horde of zombies attacks large trucks, hoping to dine on humans.*

come from, says, "You can tell a zombie when you see him. His eyes are dull and glazed, he gives no sign of recognition to people he once knew, he moves slowly and ploddingly at his tasks. . . . His facial expression never changes. He is emotionally and mentally dead."[1]

What Zombies Do

While zombies' bodies appear to be alive, their brains are dead. They are not able to think or plan. They have no **will**. But that does not matter. Zombies have someone who does the thinking and planning for them—their zombie master.

A zombie master, also called a **bokor** in Haiti, is a person who turns bodies into zombies to work

as slaves. Zombie slaves can do only what the bokor tells them to do. Sometimes their work is quite ordinary—cleaning, cooking, and farming for their master. In other stories, the bokor makes them do bad things like hurting people or destroying property.

In many old stories, zombies work alone as silent household servants. Sometimes, however, zombies work in groups on large farms planting and harvesting crops. Groups of zombies, called hordes, appear in many modern zombie movies. But zombie hordes in movies do not work on plantations for a zombie master. They move about on their own trying to find their favorite food—humans! It is lucky for these humans that movie zombies are just as slow as zombies in stories—so the would-be victims usually have plenty of time to get away.

ZOMBIES AND VOODOO

Most people today know about zombies from movies. But in the early 1900s, Europeans and North Americans learned about zombies in tales and firsthand accounts from Haiti. Today, many ordinary people in Haiti believe in zombies, and many claim to have seen them. They believe that zombies are made through the magic, **rituals,** and potions of the **voodoo** religion.

Voodoo is a mixture of West African beliefs, brought to Haiti by slaves hundreds of years ago, and Catholic rituals. People who practice voodoo believe that many gods and spirits live in everyday objects. They believe that spirits can go into a person's body and take it over. They also believe that the soul can be stolen out of a person's body, causing the body to become a zombie. The word *zombie,* in fact, in the Haitian Creole language means both a captured soul without a body and a body whose soul has been captured.

In voodoo, priests called houngan (men) or mambo (women) use rituals, potions, **trances**, and charms to contact gods, heal the sick, and protect

A Haitian voodoo priestess covers a woman with mud in a voodoo ritual.

the community from evil. Bokors also use voodoo rituals—but they use them to curse and hurt their enemies, and perhaps even to steal a person's soul to create a zombie slave.

How to Avoid Being Made into a Zombie

So many people in Haiti believe in zombies that Haitians have come up with many ways to protect their loved ones from being made into zombies. One old law—Article 246 of the old Penal Code—made it illegal to turn someone into a zombie.

 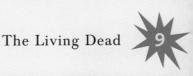

Article 246 is no longer a law, but some Haitians still protect their loved ones from being made into zombies after death. The family members may watch over a dead relative's grave for many days until they are sure that the body has started to **decompose**. Only then are they positive the body will not be dug up and turned into a zombie.

Haitians take part in a ritual to honor the dead. Many Haitians fear becoming zombies after death.

 Zombies

Families have had many other ways of making sure that their loved ones could not be made into zombies. As recently as the mid-1900s, when someone died suddenly some families would make sure the body could not be brought back to life by stabbing it or cutting out a vital organ. Other stories tell of families who strangled, injected poison into, or fired a bullet into a corpse.

Another way Haitians make sure that a body cannot be made into a zombie is to interfere with a

bokor's work. Many Haitians believe that a bokor must call a body from the grave—and the body must answer the call—before a zombie slave can be created. So, some families try to keep the corpse from responding. They may sew up its mouth with wire so that it cannot speak. Another tactic is to distract the body with silly tasks so that it will not hear the bokor. **Anthropologist** Albert Metraux describes some of these tasks: "An eyeless needle is put beside the dead body so that the dead man may spend [eternity] trying to thread it, or sesame seeds are scattered in his coffin which he will devote himself to counting one by one."[2]

Haitians sit with a departed loved one. Some believe that if a dead person is turned into a zombie, the creature can be awakened with salt.

When all else fails, and a person does become a zombie, a family can still do something to save its loved one. Haitian **folklore** claims that zombies can be woken with salt. Courlander explains: "If he [the zombie] eats salt he will either regain full life or die a merciful death. The master therefore takes great care that his zombies never have salt."[3] But salt or no salt, zombies are not disappearing any time soon. Zombies, and the stories about them, just keep multiplying.

CHAPTER 2

ZOMBIE TALES

People have been telling stories about zombies for hundreds of years. Most of these stories tell of zombie sightings, times when someone believed they saw a zombie. Many of the stories are from long ago, but some are from recent times. Some stories are told by uneducated Haitians who believe family members have been made into zombies. But others are told by doctors with many years of university training. Some stories are collected by folklorists who travel around Haiti. And other stories are told by scientists who met so-called zombies themselves.

Tales of zombie sightings have come from all levels of Haitian society, from street vendors (pictured) to doctors.

Families See Their Loved Ones

Some zombie stories tell of family members seeing loved ones long after they are dead and buried. These stories may be the result of family members wishing a loved one were still alive. But there is no way to be sure.

In one story, from 1898, a young man from the city of Cap Haitien died suddenly and his family buried him. Months later, his mother saw him working in a city street. She ran to him, but he did not know who she was. She went for help, but when she returned, he was gone. She never saw him again.

Zombies Saved

In some stories a family may actually save a loved one from becoming a zombie. These stories may simply express a family's desire to save their loved one from death itself. Or, since many people often claim to have seen the same thing, the stories may actually be true.

One such story, collected by folklorist Courlander, told of two people who had fallen asleep during a graveyard watch over the body of a young girl. They awoke to find a man removing the body from the ground. When they chased him, he escaped, leaving the girl behind, struggling to walk. She fell to the ground and gave birth to a baby. Both the girl and the baby were taken to a village

An artist shows a zombie's hands emitting an eerie glow in a graveyard.

and given salt to eat. And both of them fully recovered, much to their family's delight.

A Missionary's Story

While many zombie stories are told by Haitian families and witnesses, some accounts come from outsiders, such as the missionaries who brought

Christianity to Haiti. One such story is about a missionary who performed a funeral and burial for a young man who had fallen ill at a dance. A few weeks later, another missionary told the first that he had seen the same young man in jail in another part of Haiti. The priest visited the jail, and found the young man alone in a cell, very much alive. How the young man got from the grave to the jail is not clear from the story. But that is not unusual: Zombie stories rarely include details—such as locations or names—that would help a listener decide if a story is true or not.

Missionaries brought Christianity to Haiti. Here, Haitian women pray in a Catholic cathedral.

ZOMBIE PLANTATION SLAVES

Details are also left out of stories told by travelers to remote parts of Haiti who claim to have seen zombie slaves working in large groups on plantations—large farms that grow coffee or sugarcane. In one such tale, a traveler in the southern mountains of Haiti came upon a coffee plantation whose laborers were all zombies. They moved slowly, worked in silence, and did not sweat in the hot sun.

A traveler once claimed to see zombies at work on a coffee plantation such as this one.

 Zombies

When the traveler asked for water, no one answered. And when he tried to talk to them, the master of the plantation came with a leather whip and ordered him to leave. In this tale, the traveler explains the strange behavior of the farm workers and master by saying they are zombies. But since the exact location of the plantation is never mentioned, it is impossible to find out for sure.

RECENT ZOMBIE SIGHTINGS

In addition to the many traditional stories and accounts of zombies, there are more recent zombie encounters as well. In 1982, an **ethnobotanist** from the United States named Wade Davis traveled to Haiti to try to find out if zombies are real, and if so, how they are made. Davis met two patients in a mental hospital, whom doctors described as possible zombies.

Francina Illeus, called Ti Femme, was a Haitian woman many people thought was a zombie. She had been found wandering around a market town and had been taken to the hospital. According to Davis, Ti Femme looked and acted very much like the zombies of traditional stories. Her eyes were blank and her movements slow, heavy, and difficult.

Davis met another patient, Clairvius Narcisse, who told Davis many details about how he had become a zombie—such as the name of the hospital where he died, the location of his grave, and the name of his hometown. Narcisse also told Davis

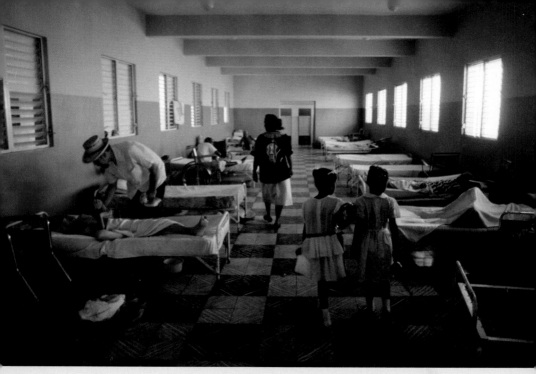

A doctor visiting a mental hospital told of two patients who thought they were zombies.

what he remembered about how he was made into a zombie.

Examining Ti Femme and Narcisse helped Davis look for answers to the mysteries of zombies. But many scientists and historians have already come up with their own ideas to explain why so many Haitians believe in zombies. They do not believe that zombies are real. But they do believe that people have very good reasons for telling stories about them.

Fear, Envy, and Anger

Some zombie stories may be rooted in envy. Since most Haitians are very poor, they often envy neigh-

bors who are rich. If people are wealthy, many Haitians believe they must have gotten their riches through evil magic—for example, by using zombie slaves to run their farms.

A fear of slavery may also be a reason Haitians tell zombie stories. For hundreds of years, Haitians were African slaves ruled by Europeans. In fact, Haiti is the only nation in which the slaves rose up and overthrew their white masters. To Haitians, the idea of becoming a zombie may express the fear of once again becoming slaves.

Many scary zombie stories first appeared outside Haiti during the time when Haiti's former

Teenagers from wealthy Haitian families enjoy a day at the pool. Some poor Haitians believe such riches have come from evil magic.

slaves took control of the government. Some people think these stories were spread by Europeans fleeing Haiti. These former slave owners may have wanted the new nation to fail so much that they spread rumors and tall tales to scare the rest of the world away.

However the stories began, many people in Haiti and other parts of the world—young and old, rich and poor, college educated and poor workers—believe that zombies exist. Their stories have made scientists wonder: Could zombies be real? Can science explain zombies? In the last two decades, many scientists have gone to Haiti to find out.

Chapter 3

Zombies Explained

Most people think of zombie stories as folklore. But some people wonder if there might be more to zombies than just folktales. Scientists from many nations have gone to Haiti to try to find out the truth about zombies.

A Medical Explanation

In 1997, British anthropologist Roland Littlewood and Haitian medical doctor Chavannes Douyon did a study of zombies for a medical journal called *Lancet*. They met three so-called zombies and found that all three were very much alive, but quite ill. One of the zombies seemed to have a mental illness that made him slow-moving and confused,

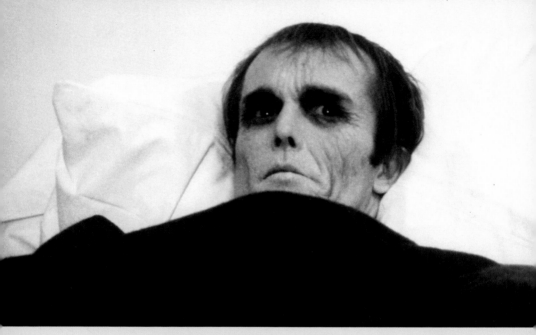

Pale and black-eyed, an actor portrays a bed-ridden zombie. Mental illness may be taken for zombie behavior by some Haitians.

while the other two seemed to have brain damage caused by disease or by alcohol abuse. Littlewood and Douyon concluded that people with mental illnesses may be mistaken for zombies in Haiti.

POWDERS AND PROCESSES

Littlewood and Douyon were not the only scientists to try to answer the question of what zombies might be. Davis also thought there might be some truth to the zombie stories. While he did not believe zombies were dead bodies brought back to life, he had heard rumors of a "zombie powder" that could turn a living person into a zombie. He wanted to study this zombie powder and meet some bokors.

In addition to meeting the so-called zombies, Davis met bokors, doctors, and families and neighbors of the zombies. He came away with a step-by-step guide to making a zombie, including the ingredients for zombie powder. Davis never actually saw zombie powder used to make a zombie, so not everyone believed he had gotten the right information. As far as Davis was concerned, though, he had finally cracked the secret of the living dead.

How to Make a Zombie

According to Davis, the first steps in making a zombie are choosing a victim—often somebody mean,

A zombie is born in Land of the Dead. *Researchers say magic and special powders are used in the making of zombies.*

greedy, and hated—and hiring a bokor. When the victim is chosen, the community acts as if that person is already dead, invisible. Then the victim is "passed the magic," or given zombie powder. Zombie powder is sprinkled over a victim's doorstep in the shape of a cross, or poured into his or her shoes or down his or her back.

The powder makes victims feel itchy. The more they itch, the more they scratch. And the more they scratch, the more the poisons in the powder enter the skin. Victims become sicker and sicker—and finally paralyzed. Barely breathing, they turn blue

Three movie zombies emerge from their graves. Once out, they become slaves to a bokor.

Zombies

from lack of oxygen. Their heartbeats are almost too soft to hear. They seem to be dead—but they are not! They cannot move, but they are aware of everything. They can hear what is going on around them.

What victims hear, according to the zombies' own stories, are the sounds of their family crying. Everyone thinks they are dead. They hear the sound of their own funeral, then the sound of shovels digging and burying their body. Later, they hear the sound of the bokor digging them up again and calling their name three times. As the paralyzing poisons wear off, the zombie is lifted from the grave, beaten, and tied up. The new zombie is now the bokor's slave.

ZOMBIE POWDER

The key to making a zombie is zombie powder, a mixture of paralyzing and mind-altering poisons. Davis met several bokors. They told him they must mix the powder carefully. Too much of any one poison would make it deadly; just enough of each ingredient makes a zombie. The bokors allowed Davis to watch while they took plants, animals, and human bones and roasted, ground, and mixed them into zombie powder. They let Davis take the powder back to his laboratory in the United States for testing. These tests gave Davis a recipe for zombie powder and an understanding of what it could do.

Zombie powder contains four main ingredients: plants or other substances that cause itching, a toad, a puffer fish, and part of a dead human body. Many other ingredients are added and some of them are **toxic**. But none are as important as these four ingredients.

Plants in the poison ivy and stinging nettle families are always a part of zombie powder. The poisonous hairs and **toxins** in these plants make victims feel itchy, causing them to scratch the skin and make small cuts. These cuts let the poisons of zombie powder get into the body. Some bokors also suggest using ground glass along with the itchy plants to irritate the skin.

Zombie powder also always contains a poisonous toad. Some toad toxins make people hallucinate, or see things that are not there. Other toad poisons make a person's heart slow down, the skin turn blue, and a victim's fingers tingle. Toad toxins do all of these things by cutting off the flow of oxygen to the cells in the body and brain.

The most important poison in zombie powder is puffer fish poison. Puffer fish—which fill themselves with water and become round and spiky when alarmed—contain a poison called **tetradotoxin**. Small amounts of tetradotoxin cause **paralysis** that lasts from a few hours to a few days. Someone who is given a small amount of puffer fish cannot move or feel pain until the toxin wears off. But he or she can think and hear.

Most bokors consider human remains to be the most magical and powerful part of zombie powder.

ZOMBIE POWDER: THE FOUR MAIN INGREDIENTS

Poisonous toads are part of the recipe for zombie powder.

Puffer fish contain a poison that causes paralysis.

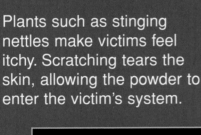

Plants such as stinging nettles make victims feel itchy. Scratching tears the skin, allowing the powder to enter the victim's system.

Human remains like this skull are a potent ingredient in zombie powder.

MAKING A ZOMBIE

1. A person is chosen to be a zombie.
2. A bokor gives the victim zombie powder.
3. The new zombie becomes the bokor's slave.

Bokors rob graves of human remains and grind up the bones, which they say are the most powerful ingredient in zombie powder.

Bokors illegally dig up old graves in the middle of the night, steal bones and other body parts, and grind them up. And while ground-up human bones probably have no real scientific effect, they do add to the Haitian public's fear of becoming a zombie.

ANTIDOTES TO ZOMBIE POWDER

Two things may reverse the effects of zombie powder. Tetradotoxin paralyzes victims by stopping

sodium, or salt, from helping the muscles move. For this reason, Davis believes that salt may be an **antidote** to zombie powder, just as the old stories suggest.

A plant called **datura,** or "zombie cucumber," is also an antidote that removes some of the effects of zombie powder so that a victim can walk. Bokors calling a zombie from the ground will sometimes give the zombie a paste made of datura. But datura is a powerful drug that makes the victim dizzy, confused, and forgetful. If it is given regularly, datura may affect the brain, making the zombie easier for its master to control.

Davis, Littlewood, and Douyon all think that zombies can be explained with science. But there is no definite proof that zombies can be created. No one has ever seen a zombie being made. But that does not matter. Most people are not interested in proof. With over 100 Hollywood movies and dozens of books about zombies to choose from, the public seems to hunger for zombie stories, true or not.

Chapter 4

Zombie Fun

Zombies have been in the public eye since the 1930s, when American troops stayed in Haiti during a period of unrest. Haiti was going through a change of government and needed American troops for assistance and security. Haiti was in the news, and zombie stories were part of the culture of Haiti.

It was not until the 1960s, though, that zombies staged a full-scale North American invasion. Americans at that time were hungry for horror, flocking to movies about werewolves, vampires, and other creepy creatures. Zombies became the next big scare.

This interest in zombies may also have reflected an interest in Haiti itself. In 1957, after twenty years of peace and wealth, Haiti came under the control of the cruel and powerful Duvalier family. The Duvaliers practiced voodoo and used gangs of thugs called Tonton Macoutes ("Uncle Bogeymen") to frighten and control the people of Haiti for 30 years. As news organizations flocked to report on Haiti, Hollywood followed suit, and zombie movies enjoyed a surge in popularity in the United States. During the Duvaliers' rule in Haiti, nearly 100 zombie movies were made. And since then, interest in zombies has never died out.

François Duvalier, pictured in 1963, ruled Haiti with brutality. Members of his powerful family were known to practice voodoo.

While zombies have been virtually unstoppable in the public's imagination, the form they have taken over the years has changed quite a bit. Zombies in folktales are created by evil bokors, but modern zombies are a whole different bag of bones. Magic and voodoo are often not involved. Instead, many modern zombies are created by science.

The New Zombie—Science Fiction Foes

Zombies in American movies and stories have often been made by some science experiment gone bad. One of the first zombie movies to become a blockbuster hit was *Night of the Living Dead* (1968). In that movie, a strange kind of beam is released from an American space probe of the planet Venus. For some reason, this beam affects the brains of all the dead bodies in the eastern United States. It makes them get up and walk. And not only do they walk, they eat—people! Great armies of zombies roam the nation, looking for humans to eat.

These zombies are very different from zombies in folklore. They are slaves to no one. They act on their own. And they are very hungry. The zombies in *Night of the Living Dead* are also different in the way they can be destroyed. Salt does not kill or awaken these creatures. They can only be stopped when their brains are destroyed.

While *Night of the Living Dead* was the first American big-hit zombie movie, it was certainly not the first movie to feature zombies, nor the last. Two

Zombies walk through a field in Night of the Living Dead, *America's first huge movie hit about zombies.*

dozen zombie movies were made in the United States before *Night of the Living Dead,* and a hundred after. And in many of these movies—such as *Return of the Living Dead Part I* and *Part II*—something in science or modern life causes the dead to rise.

In the *Return of the Living Dead* (1985), foolish workers at a medical supply company make a mistake and release a toxic gas into the air. The gas makes corpses rise up again and eat people. In *Return of the Living Dead Part II* (1988), teenagers find a barrel of toxic waste and accidentally open it up. The deadly toxin is released, once again bringing the dead to life.

Most of these modern zombies are made by accident—the result of human error. But some of the

Zombie Fun

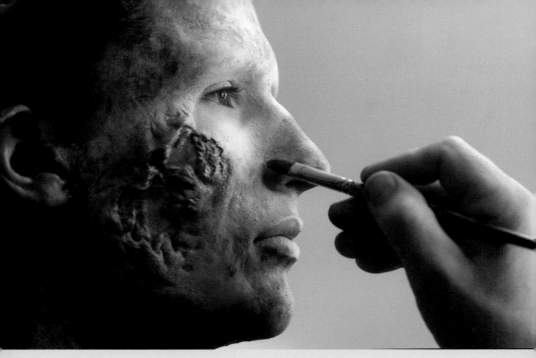

A make-up artist transforms an actress into a zombie for her role in a movie.

zombies are made on purpose—as a result of human evil. However they are made, they are modern monsters made by things that modern people fear.

ZOMBIE HUMOR

Not all zombies are scary. The zombies that pop up in children's books, cartoons, and television shows are often funny. They stumble and bumble. They are slow and confused. Their clumsiness makes them an easy target for heroes.

Scooby-Doo, the cartoon dog detective, has faced zombies more than once. While Scooby's zombies are often spooky, they are also clumsy. And Scooby-Doo and his friends always defeat the zombie and its bokor.

In some children's books and movies, zombies are victims who must be rescued. In the movie and book *Jimmy Neutron, Boy Genius,* Jimmy must rescue zombies–his parents–from their masters. In that story, all of the town's parents are kidnapped by space aliens. They are forced to wear "hats of obedience" that turn them into zombies unable to

In the movie Scooby-Doo 2, the animated dog detective and his friends encounter monsters, including a zombie (center, far right).

GOT MONSTERS?

SCOOBY-DOO 2
MONSTERS UNLEASHED

think or act on their own. Jimmy saves them by turning off the power to their computerized hats, making them free to think, act, and rebel.

Captain Underpants, the Waistband Warrior, also rescues people from being zombies in the book *Captain Underpants and the Invasion of the Incredibly Naughty Cafeteria Ladies from Outer Space* by Dav Pilkey. When space aliens pretend to be school lunch ladies and turn children into zombie nerds, Captain Underpants comes to the rescue.

Captain Underpants is not the only character who deals with zombies at school. In *The Big Nap* by Bruce Hale, Chet Gecko, a fourth-grade lizard detective, searches for the bokor who is turning his classmates into zombies. When Chet finds the bad guy, he nearly gets turned into a zombie himself.

Scary Zombie Stories

Sometimes zombies in children's books are scary instead of funny. This gives young heroes a chance to defeat an enemy. The enemy may be someone who is trying to turn a loved one or friend into a zombie. In other cases, the enemy is the zombie itself.

In the sixth Harry Potter book, *Harry Potter and the Half-blood Prince* by J.K. Rowling, for example, Harry must face the awful Inferius, zombielike corpses brought back to life by magic to do Lord Voldemort's evil bidding. In *Midnight for Charlie Bone* and other Charlie Bone books by Jenny

J.K. Rowling, pictured with her husband, holds her Book of the Year award for Harry Potter and the Half-Blood Prince, *in which Harry faces zombielike creatures.*

Nimmo, Charlie is called to rescue friends and family members who are under the spell of Manfred Bloor. Bloor uses hypnosis to turn a living person into a sort of a zombie, a person with no will, with a blank stare and empty eyes. Charlie must find a way to wake them up.

Many scary books for adults feature zombies as well. One of the most famous is by Stephen King, a master of fright. King's book *Pet Cemetery* tells the story of pets that die and come back to life, but not

Zombies provide an endless source of amusement and terror in books and movies.

quite as they were before. They are zombie pets. And when people are buried in the same grave-yard, the story gets really scary.

ZOMBIES ARE HERE TO STAY

While stories about zombies have changed over the years, they scare people just as much as they ever did. Zombies remain an unfeeling and nearly unstoppable foe, whether they are created by science or voodoo. And no matter how they change in new stories in the years to come, one thing is for certain: Zombies will not lie down and die any-time soon.

Notes

Chapter 1: The Living Dead

1. Harold Courlander, *The Drum and the Hoe*. Berkeley: University of California Press, 1960, p. 101.
2. Alfred Metraux, trans. Hugo Charteris, *Voodoo in Haiti*. New York: Schocken, 1972, p. 282.
3. Courlander, p. 101.

GLOSSARY

anthropologist: A scientist who studies people, where they came from, their cultures, behaviors, and development.

antidote: Something that fights the effects of poison.

bokor: A voodoo sorcerer who performs many rituals involving evil that most houngan will not perform.

datura (also called zombie cucumber): A plant in the nightshade family that makes people hallucinate, or see things that are not there.

decompose: To decay or fall apart.

ethnobotanist: A person who studies how different cultures use plants.

folklore: The beliefs, practices, and legends of a group of people, which are handed down through the spoken word.

folklorist: A person who studies folklore.

paralysis: The loss of the ability to move.

paralyzed: Unable to move.

ritual: The forms for conducting ceremonies.

tetradotoxin: The toxin in puffer fish that causes

the body to become paralyzed.

toxic: Poisonous.

toxins: Poisonous materials.

trances: Dreamlike mental states.

voodoo: A religion mixing African beliefs with Catholic beliefs, which involves daily contact with gods, goddesses, and spirits who inhabit the everyday world.

will: The ability to make choices and decisions.

FOR FURTHER EXPLORATION

BOOKS

Daniel Cohen, *Supermonsters*, New York: Dodd, Mead, 1977. This book is old, but it has lots of fun facts about a variety of monsters, including zombies.

Shannon Turlington, *The Complete Idiots' Guide to Voodoo.* Indianapolis: Alpha, 2002. This book has all the information anyone would ever want to know about voodoo, and then some!

———, *The Everything Kids' Monsters Book: From Ghosts, Goblins and Gremlins to Vampires, Werewolves and Zombies.* New York: Adams Media Corporation, 2002. This book contains fun information and games about zombies and other monsters.

WEB SITES

I Love Zombies (www.zombiejuice.com). This Web site lists every zombie movie made in the United States as well as movies from other countries. Readers can also learn about zombie books and comic books, and other zombie lore.

Monstrous (www.monstrous.com). This Web site has information on many different monsters, including zombies.

National Geographic News (http://news.nati onalgeographic.com). This National Geographic Web site allows readers to search for information on many subjects, including Haiti and voodoo. Includes lots of photos, articles, and facts.

INDEX

ABOUT THE AUTHOR

Cynthia Jenson-Elliott is the author of four books for children. She loves learning about other cultures and traveling the world. She lives in Southern California with her family.

"Good Heavens," said Miss Clavel, "we've brought no toy
For his excellency's little boy!"
Said Madeline, "Everybody knows, of course,
He always said he craved a horse."
In their little purses and in Miss Clavel's bag
There wasn't enough money to buy the meanest nag.

But in London there's a place to get
A retired horse to keep as a pet.

MADELINE
IN
London

Ludwig Bemelmans

VIKING-NEW YORK

VIKING

Published by the Penguin Group

Viking Penguin, a division of Penguin Books USA Inc.,

375 Hudson Street, New York, New York 10014, U.S.A.

Penguin Books Ltd, 27 Wrights Lane, London W8 5TZ, England

Penguin Books Australia Ltd, Ringwood, Victoria, Australia

Penguin Books Canada Ltd, 10 Alcorn Avenue, Toronto, Ontario, Canada M4V 3B2

Penguin Books (N.Z.) Ltd, 182-190 Wairau Road, Auckland 10, New Zealand

Penguin Books Ltd, Registered Offices: Harmondsworth, Middlesex, England

First published by The Viking Press, 1961

This edition published by Viking Penguin, a division of Penguin Books USA Inc.,

1992

10

Copyright © Ludwig Bemelmans, 1961

Copyright © renewed 1989 by Madeleine Bemelmans and Barbara Marciano

All rights reserved

Printed in China

Set in Bodoni

In an old house
in Paris

that was covered
with vines

Lived twelve little girls
in two straight lines.

They left the house

at half past nine.

The smallest one
was Madeline.

In another old house
that stood next door

Lived Pepito,
the son of

the Spanish Ambassador.

An Ambassador doesn't
have to pay rent,
But he has to move
to wherever he's sent.

He took his family
and his hat;

They left for England—
all but the cat.

"I'm glad," said the cat.
"There goes that bad hat.
Let him annoy some other kitten
At the Embassy in Great Britain."
The little girls all cried: "Boo-hoo—
We'd like to go to London too."

In London Pepito just picked at his dinner,
Soon he grew thin and then he grew thinner—

And when he began to look like a stick
His mama said, "My, this boy looks sick.
I think Pepito is lonely for
Madeline and the little girls next door."

His papa called Paris. "Hello, Miss Clavel,
My little Pepito is not at all well.

"He misses you; and he's lonesome for
Madeline and the little girls next door.

"May we request the pleasure of your company—
There's plenty of room here at our embassy."

"Quick, darlings, pack your bags, and we'll get
Out to the airport and catch the next jet."

Fill the house with lovely flowers,

Fly our flags from all the towers.

For Pepito's birthday bake
The most wonderful birthday cake.

Place twelve beds in two straight lines.
The last one here will be Madeline's.

"Welcome to London, the weather's fine,
And it's exactly half past nine."

And when they went to the place, they found
A horse that was gentle, strong, and sound.

Some poor old dobbins are made into glue,
But not this one—

Look, he's as good as new.

"Happy birthday, Pepito, happy birthday to you.

This lovely horse belongs to you."

Just then—"Tara, tara"—a trumpet blew
Suddenly outside, and off he flew
Over the wall to take his place at the head

Of the Queen's Life Guards, which he had always led
Before the Royal Society for the Protection of Horses
Had retired him from Her Majesty's Forces.

"Oh dear! They've gone. Oh, what a pity!

Come, children, we'll find them in the city."

"Careful, girls, watch your feet.

Look right before you cross the street."

Oh, for a cup of tea and crumpets—

Hark, hark, there goes the sound of trumpets.

These birds have seen

all this before.

But they are glad

of an encore.

And so are the people—on ship...

and shore.

And now it's getting really grand.

Here comes the mascot and his band.

The people below are stout and loyal,

And those on the balcony mostly Royal.

The show is over, it's getting dark
In the city, in the park.
Dinner is waiting; we must be on time.
Now let's find Pepito and Madeline.

Well, isn't it lovely—they're standing sentry
Right here at the Whitehall entry.
That is the power and the beauty:
In England everyone does his duty!

Visiting is fun and gay—

Let's celebrate a lovely day.

Everyone had been well fed,

Everyone was in his bed.

**Only one was forgotten, he'd been on his feet
All day long, without anything to eat.**

In a cottage that was thatched,
Wearing trousers that were patched,
Lived the gardener, who loved flowers,
Especially in the morning hours,
When their faces, fresh with dew,
Smiled at him—"How DO you do?"

The gardener, who was never late,
Opened up the garden gate.

The gardener dropped his garden hose.

There wasn't a daisy or a rose.

"All my work and all my care
For nought! Oh, this is hard to bear."

"Where's my celery, carrots, tomatoes,
my beans and peas?
And not an apple on my apple trees!"

Everybody had to cry.

Not a single eye was dry.

Oh, look who is lying there,
With his feet up in the air.

"I feel his breath, he's not dead yet.
Quick, Pepito, get the vet."

The vet said, "Don't worry, he's only asleep.
Help me get him on his feet.

"As a diet, there is nothing worse
Than green apples and roses for an old horse."
"Dear lady," said Miss Clavel, "we beg your pardon.
It seems our horse has eaten up your garden.

"A little sunshine, a little rain,
And it all will be the same again."
Pepito's mother said, "Quite so, quite so!
Still I'm afraid the horse must go."

Then Madeline cried, "I know what to do.
Pepito, let us take care of him for you."

"Fasten your seat belts, in half an hour
You will see the Eiffel Tower."

"Madeline, Madeline, where have you been?"

"We've been to London to see the Queen."

"At last," sighed Madeline, "we are able
To sit down without being thirteen at table."

They brushed his teeth and gave him bread,

And covered him up

and put him to bed.

"Good night, little girls,

Thank the Lord you are well.

And now go to sleep," said Miss Clavel.

And she turned out the light and closed the door.

There were twelve upstairs, and below one more.